The Mercer Stands Burning

night poems

JOHN PIETARO

atmosphere press

"A tireless fighter and organizer on the cultural front, John Pietaro now shows up with a timely volume of tightly crafted, silvery sinewed poems. *The Mercer Stands Burning*—Congratulations! I found John through his prose, his brilliant chronicling of writers of the 1930s. Later, I met and collaborated with him through the Dissident Arts Festival he's produced for over a decade"

- **Raymond Nat Turner**, performance poet, political activist, Poet-in-Residence *Black Agenda Report*. He leads acclaimed jazz/poetry ensemble UpSurge!NYC with wife and partner Zigi Lowenberg

"John Pietaro's words are soul cries, and observations, from a Real Human longing for light...like the moan of a saxophone in the NYC pandemic isolation night! Blessings, Poet Brother, on Your Excellent Book!!!"

- **Billy Lamont**, poet/spoken word artist, has engaged in collaborations with alternative rock musicians and released several albums and multiple poetry collections; his latest book is *Ripped from a Soul Still Bleeding*

"Whether penned in a tavern or cafe, or at home with the midnight oil burning...in Park Slope or Bay Ridge, in Greenwich Village, or in Woodstock...John Pietaro's poetry is infused with power, passion, and poignancy. At times glaringly gritty, then sensual and surreal, his work is as hot as a smoky jazz club, as cool as a Coltrane solo. In 'The Poet's Constellation,' Pietaro writes 'The Words...The Words...Daring to bring on the written revolution.' It's a revolution he is leading. Like Hemingway, he sits down at a typewriter and bleeds."

- **Patricia Martin**, author, poet and communications professional, Patti has engaged in performance poetry and theatre throughout New York's Hudson Valley and Torrington, Connecticut where she founded the Speakeasy coffeehouse series.

ACKNOWLEDGMENTS

The Mercer Stands Burning is for Laurie, who never fails to inspire my life's next chapter. And it's also dedicated to New York, home.

A special thank you goes to Amina Baraka, the first writer to insist on calling me a poet even when I thought it wasn't warranted---based on the rhythm, cadences, passion, and expression in my prose. She is a profound inspiration. My greatest appreciation, too, is for Ron Kolm who enthusiastically believed in my work and admitted this book into the Downtown Archives at New York University and SUNY Buffalo. And I must also give a shout out to Paul Buhle who first contacted me some twenty years ago in response to my cultural articles in the *Peoples Weekly World* newspaper, offering heartening incitement. We have since engaged in collaborative efforts which I cherish.

Widely, *The Mercer Stands Burning* is dedicated to the literary leftists, downtowners, jazzbos, punk rockers, avant gardists, night people and underground dwellers who've always guided my hand and steadied my conceit. Among them (in no particular order), Bertolt Brecht, Ernest Hemingway, John Reed, Langston Hughes, William Burroughs, Amiri & Amina Baraka, Sonia Sanchez, Nelson Algren, Patti Smith, James Baldwin, Rod Serling, Edna St. Vincent Millay, Allen Ginsberg, Jayne Cortez, Kenneth Fearing, Diane DiPrima, Steve Dalachinsky, Arturo Giovannitti, Walter Lowenfels, Michael Gold, Anne Waldman, Conrad Aiken, Richard Hell, Cornell Woolrich, Saul Bellow, Joe Hill, the John Reed Club, the League of American Writers, the Harlem Renaissance, the Beats, the Fugs, the Black Arts Movement, the Last Poets, the Unbearables.

CREDITS

"For Repelling Ghosts" was first published in *Unlimited Literature Magazine*, December 2020

"When Reagan was Bad", "The Front" and "The Bitter Early Frost" were first published in Heroes Are Gang Leaders *Gianthology,* October 2020

"The Remaining" was first published in the anthology *Father and I* (Wingless Dreamer), June 2020

"Cold Currents", "Still Winds" and "Becoming One" first published by the InterArts Collective, YouTube, June 2020

"Illegal" was first published by *Headline Poetry Press*, April 2020

"A Fallout Unspoken" was first published in the anthology *Poems from the Lockdown* (UK: Willowdown), April 2020

"With a Wicked Certainty" was first published in *The Rye Whiskey Review*, March 2020

"Langston" was first published by the International Human Rights Arts Festival, September 2019

"Burroughs Inferno", "The Lonely" and "Paved with Gold" were first published in *Harbinger Asylum*, Spring 2019

--Many thanks to photographer Sherry Rubel (SherryRubel.com) for photo of Pietaro--

CONTENTS

FOREWORD

I can still recall the scents, beer and bar food mostly, ruminating that night at a favorite neighborhood spot. It was a Saturday and I was out with Laurie Towers, my much better half, for a late dinner. Sitting in the crowded pub, we ordered our second round and the waitress, in singsong Irish lilt, invited us to the St. Patrick's Day party occurring a couple of days later. Count us in. And make mine a double.

Meanwhile, at our corner table, we were finalizing plans for that month's edition of West Village Word, my nascent poetry/music series at Café Bohemia. Still riding high from the powerful debut two weeks prior, headlined by Puma Perl & Friends, we were over the moon about the upcoming edition: a Cecil Taylor birthday tribute, a mass Women's History Month blowout led by Laurie, and a special opening set by jazz drummer Ronnie Burrage reading poetry of his late grandfather, Allan David Mahr. By the time Laurie's martini and my Manhattan arrived, all seemed good in the world. Well, not really. There was this thing called coronavirus working its way through Seattle, but from our seats in Bay Ridge, Brooklyn that night, the 2800-mile buffer felt secure. Two days later, everything changed.

The virus moved rapidly on a virulent, baneful path, followed by the noxious and malingering response of our federal government. As I write this Foreword, neither the effects nor tenacity of covid-19 are over. Not by far. Frightening numbers have been taken and the death toll across country still rises. Many remain unemployed, with lives disrupted and families facing potential homelessness. Even we who were spared of illness have seen a profound physical shift in our midst, with businesses shuttered and commercial byways, ghost towns. Nightclubs, theatres, auditoriums and other performance spaces, the heart of culture—here and everywhere--are closed indefinitely, paralyzing the arts and closing out professions in the creative community. As a live music critic, I'm currently attempting to make do with remote concerts in support of both artists and venues. But as a performer, a spoken word artist and musician, and surely as curator of West Village Word and other events, the outlook remains misted in haze, like the late summer night in which I compose these words.

In the first weeks of lockdown, my day job in the labor movement was largely modified into a work-from-home position. No one was really going out and as a means to battle cabin fever, I delved into writing, considerably deeper than usual. *Smoke Rings*, my poetry chap book, was launched late last year, but I'd maintained a good number of other pieces in reserve. I initially sought to roll them all into a full collection, but in the rush of emotions, new poems just kept coming up. Some of these focused on this new reality, including the growing political agitation I felt with each monosyllabic, self-centered utterance by the current White House occupant. And then I began to concentrate on the virus's effect on this city and my place within it.

New York has been experiencing a slow, painful shift over decades, gentrification, most often as a result of vampiric real estate developers. The Village (both East and West) has been hit especially hard, with the displaced poor and working-class as well as many of the most relevant arts spaces falling victim. Of the latter, we night people have had to brace ourselves about the loss of such cultural spaces, but creatives have always found a way to alternative locations. Now, the closure moved in rapidly and with no warning. Suddenly, the busiest of downtown thoroughfares--St. Mark's Place, Avenue A, Allen Street, 7th Avenue South, Bleecker Street, Bowery, Houston Street, lower Broadway, West 4 Street, Avenue B, Lafayette Street, Prince Street--became almost entirely immobilized. What better topic, I thought when writing this book, than our iconic, buzzing, shimmering and suddenly bleeding organism. And so, *The Mercer Stands Burning*. This collection spans many moments, emotions, experiences and visions, new and not so new, however, the underlying connection is indeed the place.

The latest addition, "When Reagan was Bad", was finished on August 14, not long before hitting the Atmosphere presses. A rather epic piece, it probes at the dark, concealed malfeasances of the Reagan presidency, viewed as a precursor to Trump. I was inspired by reading yet another book on Reagan-era censorship of artists-- particularly those involved in AIDS activism—invoked as he simultaneously slashed social services and played footsie with the so-called Moral Majority. I turned 18 in 1980 and voted against Ronald Reagan, my first formal act of dissent, and became an activist in opposition to everything "the great communicator" stood for. Little has changed. I composed this poem in bed, working late, writing with the astronaut pen Laurie bought me for just such literary emergencies, stopping finally at 4:28AM. She'd have killed me upon realizing I was up so long, but luckily, my bride is a deep sleeper.

Another recent piece, "Stripping the Dawn", however, is far removed from this kind of frustration, though it may indicate mild writer's psychosis. Completed in July, it was grown from a bit of flash fiction, "Coda", which in turn was developed from an earlier poem. In any case, it depicts a lone novelist at his desk on New Year's Eve, rushing against the turn of the calendar to make deadline. The work is completed at midnight, just as the city comes alive with blaring New Year festivities--which the protagonist accepts as laudatory congratulations for his achievement. There's a special freedom in crazy, I suspect. After a final read through, I decided it must be dedicated to one of my literary icons, Ernest Hemingway.

"Shadow People in Waiting: A Threnody Downtown" was written April 29, 1:50AM, and speaks to struggling downtown not as landscape portraiture, but a symbol of the challenges posed to creativity itself. To its author, this is a particularly relevant piece; it's where the book title was drawn from. The Mercer Arts Center which in its brief lifetime united proto-punk music, renegade theatre, radical poetry and experimental arts, rather infamously collapsed 47 years to the day (Aug 3) of this Foreword's commencement. But it's the Mercer as an emblem, a motif of the New York arts underground which I cite. The Mercer's symbolic ghost stands, embedded in the fire this time, its passage marked by capital's ashen pursuit and covid's rancor.

I wrote "A Fallout Unspoken" on April 4, 2:35am, week three of the lockdown. My first piece directly addressing the virus (and the cabin fever), it exposes my frustration and sadness as well as my attempts to fight off the very real, growing despair. The piece was published in an international anthology, *Poems from the Lockdown*, some weeks after I submitted it for consideration. And "The Bitter Early Frost" was another work of these covid days, albeit one rooted in a childhood dream I've never forgotten: discovering the body of an unfamiliar boy in a desolate area. However, this vision of death before one's so-called time linked this dream and the covid deaths neatly together, even as it conjured increasing memories of the AIDS crisis.

The ruthless advance of dementia on my father, now 91 years of age, is reflected in both "The Remaining" and "Shine, Shine, Shame". The former was composed during his first hospitalization in early 2019 when symptoms of confusion and disorientation first became profound. The latter piece was begun in the margins of my field notebook in July 2019 as I sat in a hall at the New School, reviewing a seminar of the Creative Music Studio. Ironically, the review was never published, but when the seminar closed, I walked through Greenwich Village in the extreme heat to find a restaurant for dinner and a place to write. It was a Friday, after 5pm and each eatery was thoroughly crowded with revelers welcoming in a summer weekend. One spot, however, sported outdoor seating that few dared to occupy as the thermometer bubbled in the upper 80s, but I bared the heat, desperate to finally just sit. Awaiting my meal, I alternated between a glass of ice water and a bourbon on the rocks, though my focus was painfully set on my father. By the time I was ready to hop back on the subway to Brooklyn, the piece was finished. A read through will illustrate my torn emotions, guilt over my father's placement in a nursing home and the growing resentment I felt for Alzheimer's Disease, for my family and, yes, myself.

The unexpected death of my mother on May 21 of this year is impressionistically sorted out in "The Stark, Bleached Whiteness". As we watched my father's painful decline and prepared ourselves for the probability of his passing, the months of illness and then recovery for Mom indicated a positive trajectory. No one was prepared for this turn of events. The poem recalls another unforgettable dream dating back to early childhood, one in which my mother and I were in a house she identified as having belonged to her maternal grandmother—someone she'd in reality never met, who'd died in an Italian institution. In that dream, we were searching for something never identified, rummaging in a boarded-up attic filled with sheet-covered furnishings, at the center of which stood a large, frightening animal-like statue. As much as the poem draws on this faint, long-ago vision, it also calls on the complex of emotions experienced during my mother's passing and the gray, confounded, disjointed days which surrounded it.

I feel the need to add some clarification here: this collection is not intended as funereal, I promise, though parts of it call on emotions dealing with loss of various kinds. "5:03AM: Nocturne for Steve Dalachinsky" is for the late, great poet, jazz critic and raconteur. On the night of September 15, 2019, word spread quickly of Steve's sudden hospitalization; the reports coming in went from bad to dreadful as night evaporated into very early morning. Laurie and I had a largely sleepless night, tossing, turning and pondering Steve comatose in a hospital. He'd had a sudden stroke during a performance on Long Island and was rushed to the nearest emergency room. According to his wife, poet and artist Yuko Otomo, while awaiting the ambulance Steve declared that he must have "O.D.'d on too much Sun Ra". That was Steve. The next morning, we mournfully heard that he'd passed at 5:03AM, and I knew that I had to compose this piece for him. It was written that day and completed by 11:52pm. Steve's official memorial was a bittersweet all-day celebration at Artists Space on January 19, with performances of free jazz, poetry, stories and film screenings featuring most everyone on stage, with many more filling the seats and floors of the jammed house. Premiering the poem at this event while photos of Steve were projected on screens behind me was a deeply prideful thing.

"Dancing to Incessant June: for Bern Nix" is for the celebrated guitarist who'd worked with jazz revolutionary Ornette Coleman over a dozen years. When Bern died suddenly in June 2018, I wrote a memorial prose piece for *the Wire*, the UK experimental music magazine. Not long after, my article was shared with the audience at the first Bern Nix Jazz Festival in Elizabeth NJ; by the sophomore gathering, I was asked to compose and read a poem for the occasion. I wrote the work in one sitting at an outdoor café in Bay Ridge, August 23, 2019, ending just after 11pm, performing it five weeks later at the Festival. The keynote performer, guitarist Charlee Ellerbee, Bern's partner in the dual-guitar line-up of Coleman's Prime Time Band, was available to collaborate with me for the performance, a true honor. Charlee's music wrapped around my words and cadences with soaring lines of improvisation, magical shading, aural colors and expansive, glorious harmony.

While there are further works depicting the faces of struggle, such as "And She was No More", commentary on the new rise of homelessness, and "Of Bleeker and Beyond" (dedicated to Bertolt Brecht) which speaks to gentrification's toll on the Lower East Side, there are also those set in earlier time periods. "Illegal" portrays my great-grandfather's foray to these shores, a stowaway on a freight ship. He was ultimately arrested and inducted into the US Army for service in World War One as a means toward citizenship. Several years later, he returned to Italy to bring his family over; "Paved with Gold" imagines he and my great-grandmother's somber journey to the port of New York, she a depressed, possibly schizophrenic woman who'd already spent months in an asylum in rural Italy, and would later return there in finality.

Skipping ahead over decades, "Coney Island Beach, June 1959" was inspired by family tales of my parents' first date (though this actually happened in 1953), and "Now's the Time That Wasn't", written primarily at the Applejack Diner on Broadway, depicts a 1981 bus ride up 6th Avenue into midtown Manhattan. Some timeless stories made it into this volume too. "Let's Meet at Lowenfel's" features a historic diner as sentinel; "Max of 10th Avenue" is an aging porn dealer holding forth in a dusty west side office, while "The Late-Night Breakfast Special" is served in a mythic eatery in Boerum Hill Brooklyn (though it was written at the Long Island Restaurant in Brooklyn Heights), and "The People of Night" are but background to the noir imagery that haunts New York. I dedicate this one to Cornell Woolrich; it was premiered by Puma Perl at Lady Stardust, East Village, Nov 26, 2019.

There are also poems about the artform itself: "Seven Questions" (composed in a tavern, West 33rd Street), "Sacred Room and a Typewriter" (an imaginary gaze into Dylan's studio above Café Espresso, Woodstock NY, that summer just before his career broke), "Such Lost Hands" (an imaginary poet doing time on the grisly prison labor detail of Hart Island), "Burroughs Inferno" (written in Junior's Restaurant), "Langston", "The Poet's Constellation", "Repelling Ghosts" (dedicated to both '30s writer Kenneth Fearing and '70s painter Jean-Michel Basquiat), "Words Shaped onto the Hollow", and an ironic glance at the downtown onyx-toned uniform, "A

Peripheral Haunting".

As a writer who has never stopped being a musician, sound features greatly into this collection. Some pieces were written listening to music at considerable volume, producing "Dancing 'round my Atom Fire" (inspired by Woody Guthrie's anti-war, anti-bomb "Atom Dance"), "Blue" (dedicated to the Miles Davis Sextet's immortal album *Kind of Blue*), "Impressions for John Coltrane" (all Trane, all the time; written largely at the Brooklyn Firefly), "The Lonely" (Ornette Coleman's "Lonely Woman" was on repeat, but this is also for the women's marches since 2016), "Sonic Incursion" (the music of the Sonics jolts blissfully, but while writing this, news of 13th Floor Elevators singer/guitarist Roky Erickson's death was reported), and "Chordal Clouds and Whispers" is about the music of Ran Blake. Truth be told, if I allow myself to fully escape into music-based poems, I'd fill books. Presently, the last is "Robert Quine on the Rocks" which began life at the Commonwealth Bar in Park Slope, Brooklyn, but was largely written later that night as I immersed myself in recordings of this late guitar master who shaped the music of Richard Hell and Lou Reed, the link among punk, free improv and post-modernism.

Three of the poems were a collaborative effort with photographer/filmmaker Sherry Rubel and pianist Chris Forbes, the InterArts Collective. "Cold Currents" is a reflection on the depth of the Atlantic, "Still Winds" was a covid-inspired work examining the long track of the virus, and "Becoming One" was composed in tandem with the children of Sprout U, where Sherry had collected statements which I carefully shaped and built stanzas around. The latter occurred at the height of the Black Lives Matter protests, evidenced by the esteemed, urgent responses of the kids.

Another category of poetry herein is pure political commentary. "Save for the Pride" and "A Simple Declaration" were composed in April and December of 2019, respectively. Not much reading between the lines is required. "Operation: Control", spurred by the border-detained families separated by ICE, with even very young children locked in cage-like rooms apart from their parents. This brutality is sickeningly reminiscent of earlier authoritarian attempts to dehumanize the 'other'. And "The Front", a recent, rad piece, is dedicated to writer and revolutionist John Reed. However, "Behind the Wall" dates to approximately 1991 when I was employed as a NYC HIV/AIDS Services case manager. A client, Lydia, was experiencing AIDS dementia and psychosis, believing that there were people living within the walls of her high-rise apartment. She became ravaged by the illness and paranoia. During my next visit, she was distraught and refused my entry, shouting hysterically that she had a gun. This required calls to the NYPD which notified its Emergency Services tactical unit. Within minutes the streets were filled with a phalanx of cop cars, ESU vans, ambulances, fire trucks, everyone. Lydia, barricaded in a back bedroom, ended up having no weapon and I then accompanied her to Kings County Hospital's psych ER. Such experiences led me to writing a number of AIDS-based poems as well as two full song-cycles about the people and the anxious, agitated times.

Lastly, this book harbors works simply based on time's passage and in turn, my own aging. "Of Seconds and Shadows" addresses the all too rapid bygone and serves as the title and theme of a novel I've been working on for several years between deadlines and other projects. If the style of this piece feels markedly different than the rest, it is; I wrote it in the guise of Reed Goldtran, my invented poet jailed on Hart Island in the early 1900s. He keeps popping up in my short stories as well. Can't keep a good ghost down. Others in this category include "Reels Long Lost", "To Barter with Night", "The Gloating Reflection" (which speaks, too, of the artist's penchant for self-involvement), "With a Wicked Certainty" (another noisy bar in Bay Ridge), and "Gone Again", the story of my solitary excursion to Wurtsboro NY where my paternal grandparents, decades earlier, owned a house . And the closing piece, "The Continuum", was initially a bookend poem to "Of Seconds and Shadows".

However, not everything about the passage of time is a hardship. Lengthy relationships that have evolved into beautiful partnerships, those--rare and few—are to be cherished and revered. This summer, Laurie and I marked 32 years of marriage, though we became a couple some 10 years before that. She's the love of my life, my dearest friend, my partner and best critic. Laurie's very essence begat "Silent Seconds, Tender, Stark", "Relentless" and "Breathe".

Ah, to be a writer.

-John Pietaro,
Brooklyn NY
August 23, 2020

Seven Questions

The driven pen,

Lithe, fleet, beyond relent,

Tours on forays abiding,

Bearing ancient tongues.

The course of empathy is matched

Only by the spurred charge

To absorb,

To distill,

To render oblique.

Cast, sojourner,

So transient be your berth.

-November 8, 2019, 3:45 PM

Stripping the Dawn (for Ernest Hemingway)

In the small of a darkened room,

The one lighted by laptop,

He sat.

Icy snowfall pelting windows

This late December night, but none heard.

He typed, racing, as the calendar awaited its turning.

        The space was chilled, barely tolerable,

         And this only led to faster work, faster,

      Forging the drama, scenarios of the overheard, the
                       miscast,

          And whispers.

Unending, this day.

And then it vengefully took on dusk

And bled the hours.

Guy Lombardo's five saxophones hovering above

Sought to warm, heavy on vibrato, and

The Waldorf shimmered in four-color animation.

                       CHARACTERS.

      The characters are but ghosts of fading percepts,

      Stained of past and passerby, they ring and linger,

          The breadth of then or never,

                    The reach is far.

               Conjured, cast, spiritual glistening of want.

Listening from within. That's something writers do.

The muse sparks under bright lights, caustic sound,

Heavy traffic, and barroom din, but realized in haze.

The pen arouses the dregs,

Conceiving the essence,

Cleaving the soul.

                    Raven, the arcane night filled the room,

                    His eyes radiant by the candor of glare.

                    Drawn, now, he, to the final page,

               His final page, hardly his own image. Perhaps.

                    Head back, he released a throbbing laugh

                         Breaking the night as

Passing car horns expressed into holiday air.

And there was shouting and exultation.

His downtown walk-up shook as

Fireworks lit the skies over Manhattan.

Times Square has assuredly caught on,

Lauding him, applauding him,

Pouring out congratulations for a once private victory.

                         He ran to the window, then,

Throwing it open,

Raising a hand to the throngs,

Welcoming the adulation,

Aglow.

Saturation to the vivid, the revelers awry

With the vaguest notion of to be.

Stripping the dawn, this...

This coming of the new.

-July 23, 2020. 11:12 PM

A Fallout Unspoken (week three, lockdown)

The air about us in

The coming of Spring

Feels a little more still now.

A bit more static,

Almost solid.

Gray, it hangs low, this

Concrete sky.

Impenetrable,

It casts silence over

The city that can't seem to wake.

Sullen city

Doesn't know where to turn.

Living herein,

Standing afar, it's

Whispers lie dormant.

And the pall that holds us

We thought would arrive with

Howling boom and argent glow

Carries instead

A fallout unspoken.

-April 4, 2020, 2:35 PM

Shadow People in Waiting: A Threnody Downtown

One with the streets, a
Haunting by name,
Reflections seek sky
After the rain.

Downtown byways,
Long shadows throw time,
Eastside Lilliput
Old residues rise.

Forlorn as noon day,
The visions tossed
Through passage of rite,
Eternity's loss.

Long orphaned works
Of film, pen and brush
And razor-sharp voice
Of theatre unsung.

Of here nor there
So luminous, I,

Seeking the Once
In purple-black nights.

Now tacit the shells
That lie in the wait;
Call for the turning,
The progress of rakes;

The haunt of No Rios
Tin palaces still shine,
The Mercer stands burning,
The gourmand divine.

Now cinemas transgress
Wherever they lay
Kill idols and darlings,
So mortal the day.

"No vacancy" ensigned o'er
Alphabet Lane,
Unbridled the wanting of
Two hands catching rain.

-April 29, 2020, 1:50 AM

5:03 AM: Nocturne for Steve Dalachinsky

3:15AM. Shhh. Speak nothing now.

Speak not.

There's a fading din beneath the well of silence.

It turns envious the darkling.

The sun now rises later than it once did,

Doesn't it?

4:37. September's torrid dampness cedes to nothing

Here in Brooklyn, but

The chill of the Long Island Sound

Freezes the poetry in time, like

Burroughs in Morocco,

So far from home.

4:55, this day which bordered no sleep,

Mind festering, precious pain.

The sun must rise later than it once did.

Tell me it does.

The call of gulls falls deaf on hospital walls,

Where strange machinery turns, tabulates,

And sways through

Cross-rhythms of tap, scrape,

And sob.

A dancehall of wire brushes ignites

Booming skins and shimmering bronze,

Gassing the flame of sauntering yesterday,

As after-hours haze covets

A thicket sound in vivid black

Downtown.

The call of Gayle in the wild, he, Streets the Clown

Seething through tubes and drips, submerged in

The unfettered, busking improvisation.

And the final night erupts joyously leading you

South of Houston.

The colors, the shapes which fall from your pen

Cast a reflection of then into tomorrow.

Many tomorrows,

Poet Laureate of Outside.

5:03AM. The sun halts in its place, as

The mist purples

Over Spring Street.

And the clouds are but a

Painted backdrop.

-September 16, 2019, 11:52 PM

Sacred Room and a Typewriter (in Woodstock NY)

Hot sky, clearest woods,

Closing eyes, I blow down 28,

A harsh cut into magical roads as

Both sides embrace the hollow. Both sides

Embrace

Green earth, scent of new,

Mountain tops scrape the clouds,

Billowing over, the soft self

Left only its best devices. Only its

Only.

Curved path, sensuous as hips and thighs,

More alluring than city lights in Christmas skies,

Stumbles onto breathing air, a playhouse of ghosts,

Pageants past, stage icons

Tarred with poetry of pain,

Tears so just

 and

Songs of songs of

Cycles.

Pinks, reds, darkest blue,

Hearts cast astray and

The ego is only ever released over

Such special streets.

Not even the vagabond could have known.

- March 30, 2019, 12:36 AM

Such Lost Hands

In the far corner, just beyond reach,

In the bind of mist and veil

Stood the haunt of 1911:

Reed Goldtran. Poetry.

For more than a century it remained,

Waiting patiently.

Treasure-trove of a lost poet no one knew

And none recalled

---Reed Goldtran.

Name like an anagram. And the

Title, so spare, so simple,

So emergent. Like an oasis.

I'd open it at random spots, never beginning to end,

But outside in;

Before sleeping, in quiet moments,

But mostly amid writing.

And when I wouldn't heed to the book, its poetry returned

In visitations:

Time's calling and its phantoms,

Our blessing and perdition.

On Hart Island, Goldtran lived and labored in

Ashen prison and burial ground;

Into the trenches of fruitless soil with

Boxes of pine, interchanging, faceless.

Seeking sky through stone,

The poet mourned the dead,

Lamenting muses befallen

In maudlin dreams.

And Reed Goldtran

Of sordid fog and distant shore

Weaponized the words

Of such lost hands.

So, I stared into the page, seeking

something cast

In lines aged,

But the elders wouldn't speak.

The book is a doorway and

One need only trust the shadows.

- May 6, 2020, 9:40 PM

Burroughs' Inferno

The sawdust kicking up

Like sparks

Has caused

An electrical fire

Onstage.

Small, strained eyes peer through

The blackened veil of a fedora.

Cigarette loosely dangling

From lip,

His taut, lined face longs to feel.

He bleeds in verse;

Love is but the haunting melody.

It pours through transoms over

Smoke-stained rooms as

Spilled bourbon sizzles lacquer and

Cuts deep, dark, hard wood.

Crack of a rim-shot,

Cymbal sortie splits thickened air as

The tenor moans bluest mourn.

The next bass drum bomb

Tears the front row,

Summoning sirens, stirring drinks and

Reciting to fathoms below.

-January 11, 2019, 12:15 AM

Of Seconds and Shadows

Indebted to the hours, I

Who own yesterday must

Compose what's to be.

Revolution's hands

Compass youth's pass

In surge and dash and streak.

But then for the aged,

Clockworks bedeviled

By specters beyond reach.

   We reside on this plane

   Of muted mem'ries;

   Awash, who---who dares speak?

   Here is the season of

   Visions relentless,

   Misled moments of yore.

      Astray in time's eye,

      Tacitly other, drunken of

      Spirits forlorn.

In a space unseen,

The race of seconds,

Grimace of shadows

S t i l l b o r n

When Reagan was Bad

There was a time, wasn't there,

When Reagan was bad?

Real bad?

Teflon Don before there was,

His method-acted charm and B-movie grace

Arm in arm with Helms and Thurmond.

We died, laughing. We died by the millions.

Lifestyles of the Rich & Famous,

Transglobal vanities, sans savings.

No loans and, hey,

There's powder on your nose.

You've still got Milken on your lips too, don't you?

And what of Bonzo at Bitburg laying wreaths

On Mag the Knife?

Remember? Remember when?

When Reagan was bad? Real Bad?

In the throes of Fallwells and Wildmons,

Schlafly's pulpit an October Surprise

Contra-indicating the Jessicas and Tammy-Fayes

Who kneeled deep for penance.

Remember when we the people were bad, so bad they

Had to stop us? They told us so.

Remember when Edwin Mouse roared "Entartete Kunst!"

As Mothers of Prevention vamped

Moral equivalents of Founding Fathers and

D'Amato squatted, expressing all over "Piss Christ"?

You know you do.

And when Rohrbaching Frohnmayer reamed out
"Witness"

While licking chocolate off of Finley?

That Commission peered deep into Sprinkle and

Close-danced over Mapplethorpe's grave,

Their footprints piercing normal hearts,

Blackening eyes and souls to

Shutter mouths in St. Pat's,

But December first never arrived.

Just ask the angels.

Galleries burnt, then, like flags, the ashes of

Charred Reds and Jump Blues

Scattered through our veins.

Illegal needle exchange, a

Diocese of shredded dogma strayed

Like lives where social service gone expired,

Passé as voice, hollow as will.

Some remember.

Gipper, you laughed, naming dues-paying names and

Whispering into Cohns of Silence, you,

Warrior in from the cold,

Shriveled smile buffed with saddle-soap,

Dressed in diamonds on loan.

Illegal arms for trade! Illegal arms!

Step right up! Step right up!

We're mourning, we're mourning,

We're mourning all over America.

Gipper, your diaper filled with

The spill of tomorrow preserved

The shit of today...

Democracy for sale to the highest bidder.

They dug you out and propped you up with

Hollywood lights and market dregs,

These thoughtless charades combed over the rot

To cast the command performance

Fit for Narcissus. It's been 40 years, 45.

Your reign is but the shrapnel.

Remembering when Reagan was, when Reagan was…

When life fluttered over the Stock Exchange balcony,

Loose cash inciting to riot and the

Butcher's bill now calls in the payment.

A nether day.

There was a time,

That time,

One we remember.

But this day, today, we live through

Still again.

Now, Nicaragua is Mexico and

Dying queens, the new immigrants.

Conspiracies are heritage as

Charlottesville chants

"So Proud of Your Boy",

Mask-less but hooded

For blood and soil.

Day's undone.

We remember; we can't help but.

Yet, still

We die.

We die, laughing.

-August 14, 2020, 4:28 AM

Save for the Pride

Vanity's bad veneer,
Devoid by design,
Marketing fear
Cast in reflection.

He speaks in deception
Unknowingly nude and
Wielding corruption.
Bedeviled by loathe, his

Poison is wrath.
Yes, gluttony abides
On Primrose Path, it's
Forty-five.
(It's later than you think)

In lust, voters strived,
Thought be damned,
His status assigned,
Presiding orangutan

Of elfin hand,

Lost in time, G-Man is

Greed, man.

Plasticine:

You can read a magazine

Right through him.

The hollow hunts and feeds

Gorging feckless whim.

But Narcissus still cries

For unrelenting sin,

Save for the Pride,

Save for the Pride.

(It's later than you think)

-April 28, 2019, 2:34 AM

Reels Long Lost

I stirred,

And the aging floor creaked in response.

Without warning, the match blew out and,

With plumes craning upward,

A rich darkness

Engaged.

> Eyes shut, the linger of youth slowly emerged.

> The ring, the linger. Of then.

> The ring, the linger of this place.

> Alive.

> Overwhelmingly so.

> Pulsating with movement. And sound.

> Parades of sound, generations of

> Passersby.

> The ring, the linger. Of lives. Stories.

> So many stories.

Pictures in splashes came into view, looming

As if projected from 16-millimeters,

Reels long lost,

Tossing dust through the heat of

Hurtfully bright light.

> And it came rapidly, the imagery.

It came persistently, the memory.

The linger.

And I stood to welcome what once lay muted.

And She Was No More: to the forgotten

There is a din 'neath the well of silence

And it turns envious the darkling.

By birthright, transparent, she,

None could recall,

Reticent on our streets, lost in our endowment.

The food others call trash can sustain and

Glass tower canopies shelter,

But the greatest hunger is for the being.

The muted fall empty,

Echoing lessons of silences past.

Saturnine the cry, mouth begotten.

They said only the naked go hungry and

It's the mad under heartless skies.

We were told the guilty languish, and

Deprived are the faithless and shunned.

Now, the boldest lie, swallowed whole,

Groans inequity, aching desire.

And there stood a hollow

Where once was cause.

And she...

And she was no more.

-June 1, 2020, 12:20 PM

A Simple Declaration

Once,

Not so very long before, but

Once

--sometime before this, at least--

He'd come to the supreme decision that

It was no longer to be.

He'd been sure of the need

To dispense with it for some time, so

None could doubt his decision, surely not

The throngs greeting him in the weeks and months

Which followed.

Such a masterful remaking!

And

That was the very best part.

Soon thereafter, it simply never was.

Few could well recall it, anyway.

But at a later interval, for reasons unclear,

He began to quietly sing its praises.

Initially, just as nostalgia and only on special occasions.

But then the people began discussing

Having had it.

Quickly,

It was recalled only in the best possible light.

He began to champion it during speeches

And the people of course began to crave it.

With a mass campaign,

With jingles and a snappy musical review,

With decrees and proclamations and incentives,

It became all the rage,

To levels unimagined before.

His poll numbers soared and

Even the critics praised his recognition of it.

Such a masterful discovery!

Yes, that was the very best part.

When none could envision a time without it,

It was simply declared.

Declared to be.

And

He was pleased with his efforts of

The great revelation,

Proud of his toil and creation.

Waist-deep,

Who else could have borne the burden or

Sustained the heights

Of such an audacious

Declaration?

-*December 19, 2018*

Dancing 'round My Atom Fire

(After Woody Guthrie's "Atom Dance")

Heavy waters, words of wit,

G-Man made the atom split.

Trotting flaming jetson cinders,

Winged Valk'ries, clouds are lit.

Sizzling sky and blackened sea

Singing of your wanton greed

Force of eagles never hinders

Earthly weightly broken

Me

Woody always spots the liar

Dancing 'round my atom fire

Steaming cold this fallout winter

Cities melt in simm'ring pyre

Neutron never lets the noise in

Choking on your radial pois'ning

Lay us out like so much tinder

Tower smoking, profits boiling.

Blue (for the Miles Davis Sextet, 1959)

Blue. Not all blue, but blue.

    Kind of.

      Kind of Blue.

        Miles' horn cried, stretching for the sky

          Through a rayless, leaden room.

            Candle-lit, sure,

           But the dark was,

          The dark was always let in,

        Drinking in the hue of

That piano, those chords those,

Chords.

The threading network,

Sounding water-colors to paint

The hollow:

The harmony of a new day, blue way.

Miles on high.

        And sinewy, playing the music of lonesome:

            Coltrane.

      He tears twilight into a thousand after-hours and

           Countless early morns.

That lost moment
when

Even the night fly lays still.

The sky, at its blackest, then,

can only blow purple.

And ponder the blue to come.

Shattered fragments of white gold

Watch from a safe distance as

The winds die off, the

Vacuum sets in and

Urban revelers

Sleep off the residue of night.

Here in the sediment,

The sizzle and ping cast a

Picture plane of

 Jimmy Cobb's hands,

Dancing inwardly, utterly to

Mr. PC's walking, widening, wooden pulse.

Cannonball sings,

Sings old,

Sings out and new,

Pulling the gospel from his horn, but,

But its Coltrane that lights the night.

Sheets of beauty, sheets of

Pride, sheets of soul

Crucified.

But Evans,

His pain for the rest to mourn.

Evans, that piano, those chords those,

Chords,

Muted tapestry, and aural prism

Cast sorrowful polychromes

Over heartless chasms.

The harmony of a new day, blue way.

And Miles sighed.

-January 21, 2019, 2:53 AM

Langston (for Mr. Hughes)

The poet sings of rivers.

Standing at mountain's edge,

He stares down the sky and

Embodies the pain of a people.

The poet mourns his testament

But never his words,

Bearing phrase, rhyme and couplet

To cleanse the very language.

The pen carves out his reality,

Raining messages of hope and lament as

One,

Lacerating boundaries

Fluently

As drawing

Sword from stone.

-January 10, 2019, 9:57 PM

The Lonely

Inspired by Ornette Coleman's "Lonely Woman", and the 2016 Women's Uprising

There was no sound,

The long moment embraced by a falling grayness.

And a hush silenced her very breath.

And she remained motionless.

    Bronze ring of ride. And again, and again, and again.

Bass groans lingering stillness within its joyful noise and

        It becomes the dance relentless.

Uptempo push and retreat turns the clouded lament onto
itself.

        And she remained motionless.

The cry of centuries, the darkness of lonely.

The woman crosses left hand to right shoulder

And bows her head, sullen,

Caressing the mystic silence.

        All is found within,

        Within the emptiness.

        Held aloft in transparent movement,

        A sudden pulsation, a rush in rhythm,

        That simply overwhelmed.

The mourn of millennia, the madness of quarry.

The woman, crossed eyes calling out despair,

Lifts her head, searching,

Rejecting the vague wantonness,

The hollow in thy name.

- January 27, 2019, 2:10AM.

Cold Currents

Darkest waters

Course the ocean floor,

An eternity of sand submerged within

Blind cliffs and valleys.

They mock the deserts and

Void the sky.

There are hidden lives and ancient myths

Far beneath the violence of tides;

Here is eternal night.

Ghosts of

Vessels forgotten and

Spirits befallen ride,

Ride the cold currents, the

Bitter winds carrying

Silent cries.

-June 7, 2020, 2:58 AM

Now's the Time That Wasn't

Almost 6:50 PM, thickening gray as,

The blue above melts black.

The clatter of New York streets

Splattered web of lights sporting

The metallic sheath heading uptown.

This happens to be 1981 and everyone says that traffic is as
bad as it could ever get.

...The bus door opened—*ker-rrrap*---and I clumped up the
stairs,

Pausing for a moment to fish for a token.

The bus wheezed asthmatically forward, fighting the tide.

And the streets lumbered on.

The avenue surrounds the bus,

Gripping vengefully.

The buildings larger, closer and

Neon burned brighter as

Dusk blankets the autumn sky.

There's something in the dark.

You never make the light at 42nd;

It's always red when you arrive, but

This offers a view of hallowed ground.

Theatres of the wanton, land of the lost,

Glitter beneath stain, and

Glory begone

Begone.

The preachers and the buyers,

The dealers and night riders,

The buskers and beggars and the
forgotten.

And I smell the skies over Times Square sizzle and burn.

Sonic Incursion

Remembering Roky Erikson and celebrating the Sonics

Sonic incursion,

Imploding wave conversion,

The grip of fallout descending.

Vibrato spits electric,

Commanding breath, burning lung:

The pain primal.

And all that is, is loosed upon.

> *Oh, carry me to my*
>
> *Distortion goddess,*
>
> *Carry me distant,*
>
> *Inside is out*

Larynx shreds guttural saxophone;

Inflamed amplified sound fission.

Drums howling, splashing abandon,

Cymbals drown in sweat,

All pulsations liberated, home today.

House afire pours black mist upward

Painting skies rayless.

> *Oh, carry me breathless to my*
>
> *Distortion goddess,*

Carry me further,

To the far side of myself

The tight leather bands restraining

Bonneville's Bad Betty, cutting deep deliciously,

Only withhold restraint itself.

This is the tender music of shattered windows and

The great unmuffled. It speaks of

Yesterday, tomorrow, nevermore.

Miss me.

Oh, carry me to the holiest

Distortion goddess,

Carry me out stoned, starry-eyed

And straight jacketed

The long tracks to nowhere

Endless path of the unkind,

All that is, is the road ahead.

Screams of strychnine

And abandonment.

Loveless, loveless, loveless.

Will travel.

Must.

-June 5, 2019, 12:50 PM

The Remaining

It had been a long, slow pursuit toward

Detachment.

And then the decline rushed him vengefully.

His clipped street baritone now a hoarse,

Rustling tenor of scant endurance,

Repertoire lost.

I spoke, he looked on.

Nimbly, he traveled. From empty to away.

Empty to away.

I rolled this phrase silently over lips and tongue,

In a whisper softer than my father's, almost a
mouthing.

He didn't look back this time.

From empty to away.

An ebb, a melt, a razing, a striking. An erasure.

I stared into his face, absorbing it.

The erasure is always chasing us down,

Seeking to bring us to away.

To away.

Our struggle is in the remaining.

-Feb 12, 2019, 1:01 AM

To Barter with Night

Amidst the day,

As hours exchange

Sleep for want,

I barter with night,

Partaking of the sky.

It hangs there, aloft,

Blue and billowy white.

Golden center,

Warming over

This odd winter hour.

Tender the moments

'neath the call of dusk.

And Brooklyn

Hasn't painted this scenic

Since just before the shearing.

-Jan 24, 2020, 4:15 PM

Paved with Gold

Miguel and Antoinette arrived during a storm
A storm that blew like broken glass
Over the Atlantic.

New York on the far edge of autumn
Made no allowances for the weary or the cold;
Its frigid dampness smiled no welcome.

"The line is so long. So long", she said.
Slowly, he switched his gaze from
The endless line before him to his wife and

Her pallor of skin,
Concealed mouth,
Widening black eyes,

Vapid; the empty veneer of
A discarded doll.
"So very long", she repeated softly.
"So very", now more of a faded whimper.
He offered no answer,

His expression unmoved.

The emptiness only allowed the sickening back in.

The hum of whispering voices in many tongues

Only taunted.

The Gloating Reflection

The leaden downpour allowed

No visibility, and

Late summer's heat clung insistently to the windows.

I slowed the car to a crawl as sudden flashes bore

A distant howl.

Navigating the cubist landscape, broken only

By a frantic dance over glass,

The car came to a merciful, slow halt.

Eyes wide, seeking dry land through colorform shapes

Within the streams,

Within the shadows of the streams,

Snaking, coiling, roiling,

Over and through as

The gloating reflection

Melted from view.

Another crack of thunder tore

The purpling sky.

Shine, Shine, Shame

Shine, shine, shame;

Shine, shine, shame;

You left your father in the rain,

    You left your father far behind.

    Shame, shame, shine;

    And when did he recall the times?

    Where was he when first resigned?

    Last to sign.

    Shine.

        Who, but who is he beside?

        Where is he, but without?

        Without and withered, when?

        When?

            Withered.

Withered. When.

  Spirit spent, Friday's sent

    Reflection's shame: you left, you left

    Left your, left our, left my

    Father duly spent—

      I turn my head, you belch consent.

        Mindful bend, sending same,

        Sending same:

Stagelights blue, closing
game.

Purple skies paint sainted sighs,

Sainted lies on dying flames.

Shining shame,

Shackled drones of hollow homes.

Closing eyes like

Battened he,

Face begone,

Where was as and

Halcyon.

Never speak,

Ever be.

Shackled we,

Shutter game.

Purple skies paint,

Sainted lies on dying flames.

Shining
shame,

Syphoned he,

Sickened me,

We sent our father out to sea.

-July 19, 2019, 5:49 PM

Coney Island Beach, June 1959

After the film and newsreel but

Before the start of the Ronald Reagan

B-picture,

The two slipped out.

Toasting the breeze off the Atlantic

With cotton candy and leftover Jujubes,

They sat on a boardwalk bench

basking in sun's setting.

The air smelled of sea salt and Solar-Cane.

Every barker came alive

As the crowd filled the area about them.

And down in front and out from under,

Coney Island's sand horizon called out

The shore walkers, hand-in-hand,

Clam diggers and fortune hunters,

Sun worshippers unaware of ultra-violets

And overheated lovers beneath,

Unconcerned with shaded glares.

But it's the lightly clouded aquamarine sky,

Of gentlest wind,

That one needs recall in winter.

Impressions for John Coltrane

Impressions of liberation,

Proud, full-throated, full-bodied,

Force of one force sustained:

John Coltrane.

Heart ravaged, pulse asunder

As he takes the skies.

Coltrane, Coltrane

Digging through harmony like a derrick unmanned,

Tearing ground to forge

The unearthed, the infernal new,

Leaving behind ruins of sound,

The bodies of jazz past thrown from speeding black
sedans,

Chrome-blinded, windows down, the rush of air and

Dizzying view, too much to bear.

Coltrane, Coltrane.

Talisman, my bourbon, my joint,

My Bud on tap.

The far from over, the other way,

The Next...

Roiling, boiling, broiling,

Elvin, throbbing within,

The dance of four limbs

Careening, crashing tumult,

Like the silent war of cosmos

Close-miked.

But the force of horns is relentless.

Coltrane, Dolphy,

The timeless two.

Shock of the free

To never again.

Abstraction is the only reality.

It lies on a spectrum few can see,

Worlds within worlds

Without end.

-March 1, 2019, 1:21 AM

Of Bleeker and Beyond (to Brecht)

Street so dark, even as

The sun holds above.

Scent of beer and age

Fused incessant, beneath.

Passersby, faster than most,

Move on the crosspath

Of Bleecker, Bleeker and

Beyond.

The seeker descends.

An off-the-curb experience eclipsing Bowery,

End of the line, onto East 1st until it

Dissolves at Houston and

Tenements reach upward to shut the sky.

Coats of urbanity on

Canvas of brick and

Layers of self,

Far east and further,

Where the air

Stinks of change.

Where the people's blood flows

Like rivers of sound.

-March 19, 2019, 10:40PM

Chordal Clouds and Whispers (for Ran Blake)

Bathed in textures of deepest gray,

The soundtrack of sleepless nights and restless days.

Stark. So stark the touch, a distant stare

Through blackest shades.

Ran Blake's hands shape chordal clouds,

The dark of whispers, mysteries of sound.

So fluid, so wide, a searching dirge of

The bluest hour

Disavowed.

A noir for dreams and tomorrow's past,

Naked,

Smoke-filled,

Flagrantly apart,

Shadows' wrath

Tempts midtown souls and

Denizens of old onto

Horizon's winding, blind path.

-September 26, 2019, 12:57 AM

With a Wicked Certainty

The rush of sound soars past my ears

At a pace faster than seems natural.

But it's welcome.

The taste of bourbon on vermouth

Slides over my lips as

The rush of some sports event

Rings over multiple televisions in concert,

Above

And well out of gaze.

I have no idea whose playing or whether it be

Ball game, tennis match or

Horse race.

Probably not

A tennis match.

And the scent of loud pilsner

Strikes my nostrils with a wicked certainty.

-May 9, 2018, 7:15 PM

Operation: Control

As one Agent forced Mia down,

Another confined her wrists in unyielding cuffs,

And with her face pushed into arid ground,

He locked another set over her ankles,

Seething metal biting tender flesh.

Mia struggled, aimlessly howling

Like a wounded beast.

"Be careful---she's going to bite!", the Watch Commander
warned.

He placed a leather restraint over her mouth,

Pulling the twin straps across the back of her head,

Securing the buckle with a snap.

Mia's hair hanged over her face,

Mangled through the taut bands.

Her flushed cheeks and reddened eyes bulged,

Creating the appearance of something

Less than human.

Her breathless cries had no effect,

Offered no means to cease

The sickening futility,

Of confining finality.

And Mia looked one last time
Into her daughter's eyes.

The People of Night (For Cornell Woolrich)

Out of the lobby and onto the sidewalk,

The heat had finally given way to the calendar...

Where streetlamps cast gilded beams through blindness,

Clouded streams hovered, rolling slowly,

So slowly,

The mobility barely noticeable.

Low-hanging fog clashed dutifully with

Shadows tossed of hidden senses.

'Night Has 1000 Eyes'.

You can taste the lateness though

We've not yet hit the blue hour.

Standing consciously still,

I listened for the sounds of quiet and,

Distant movement, the

People of night well out of frame.

The air on the cusp of cool

Caressed silkily, sensuously, lazily,

Like the touch of Veronica Lake

Just before the snarl.

Encased in the darkling,

My eyes grew heavy.

And I became of the mist.

Dancing to Incessant June: for Bern Nix

A singular survivor of the Free

All the way until he wasn't,

Bern Nix of simply ever, where

Elysian Fields fade to the sea.

Unique among the most avant of the garde,

Fireworks of our creative core,

6-string tones of post-modern lore.

Legitimacy asunder by design.

By design.

Nix' speaking voice, too, gently urbane,

Sphynx-like repose.

A sparkle in his eyes and deft of refrain,

Talk of clocks and cosmos,

The room gently became his own.

A stage whisper—spoken or played.

Unassuming, the embers of a

Poetic No Wave.

"This music allows harmony to shift, like chase-chords"

Chase-chords, said he. Chase-chords urgently redefine

Where we've been to predict

Our "to be".

Old as King Oliver and fresh as

Fading away.

Shock of the New. Hell, yeah.

"The 'swing' was always there",

He said.

Bern could always feel the swing,

Tap his foot to the hidden agenda and

Sing the struggle for justice in

Advanced harmony.

Bern could always sense the bullshit,

Always predict the next lie.

Always drown out the power

Elite.

"This music is an extension of the early

Jazz tradition", he said,

"Where the sense of freedom, the improvisation,

Was constantly creative",

Bern always let freedom sing,
Saunter and sting
Well beyond imaginary bar-lines of liberation.
Goddamn, wasn't Bern just the thing?

"Here the band's roles are never static", he said,
"Always shifting, evolving…", said he,
"Moving through and beyond. It is in and it is out…"
IN and OUT.
Through and beyond, through
And beyond.
In and still
Out.

A place where tonality is re-cast and
Harmony a phantom of times passed.
Bern's quivering single notes,
Barked dyads and chordal runs up,
Up and down
UP and down and then across
His ax's neck,

Emitting a certain magic, a

Paying of the dues, a

Warlock's accord,

A wizardry of the blues.

Stoic, broad-stroked hues of

Elder and then,

Vagabond pallets of unconceived,

And never before, never

Again, the artful Prime of

The Time of

Gifts last received.

Toying with repetition,

Kandinsky-esque staccato,

Drip painting in anti-gravity and

Shotgun-fire,

Splashing up and

Spilling masterworks

Across the mournful sky.

Bite, lament, snarl and cry,

Bellow, he, and then swoon,

Eyes deep, like the breadth of

May's Flower Moon.

And softly

Bern danced to incessant June, but

Oh,

Oh, so softly.

-Aug 23, 2019, 11:01pm,

Robert Quine on the Rocks

It's almost dark.

In here.

With a gloved touch, the somber, open chords lazily
compel.

Scent of flight and first sip lure me into the moment.

My pen

Moves incessantly as

Joyously jaded guitar permeates even my glass.

Quine descends and laments electric as a

Subterranean pulse clouds the air.

Notebook quakes beneath my pen as

Sounds of inverted '60s surf billow over;

Plectrum on high, winding cross-fueled paths.

An aural coloring book of crushed and melted wax in

Reds, purples, custard yellow and burnt sienna.

Lines ignored and margins become fair game as his

Left hand becomes a tarantula in mid-flight.

I'd better have one more, just to be safe.

Something about his Stratocaster's pure ice.

Pained, painted twang

Sputtering, reaching, shredding, adorning.

It's a dark night dance and the distinctions

Mean nothing anymore.

-September 25, 2019, 1:35 AM

Gone Again

It was the sound of the water drew him in.

A distant, consistent, whirring, trickling,

Not quite running water.

It stood out, and demanded a presence

That day he went back.

It was the sound of the water drew him in,

Calling him almost by name.

It might have gone unnoticed, but

Upon closer listening,

There was at least a hint.

Yes.

Yes, there it was again.

A steady flow,

Orchestrated sensation.

Highs and lows that shimmer and dip,

Bubbling, humming, tickle rocks and foliage.

A sound so complete it seemed

It seemed staged for the tourists,

If there were tourists.

No, not quite running water.

It was softer.

More of a walk.

The shhhhhhhhhhhhhh of it

Most alluring.

As he tacitly moved up the road,

The sound--that sound--became more prominent.

Calling out with the certainty of current.

So cold, so clear, this tiny stream,

Languid hand of mountain rapid.

He stood on its bank,

Just to the side of mem'ry's rise.

Shhhhhhhhhhhh.....

The endless, timeless whisper

Drew him in.

He reached for another cleansing breath,

Hoping to steal the moment,

Hold close the waning seconds,

Clutch them to his breast,

But they evaded grasp,

Turned elusive and then

It was too late.

Lost for the want,

He was already gone.

Again.

The Bitter Early Frost

I was there.

He was dead.

Immobilized, I stared as he

Lay still, pallid face hollowed

By cast haze.

His eyes sealed, unseeing,

Cheeks drawn, near concave, yet

The flesh slack upon surrender.

I shouted for a friend to seek help while

I stayed with the rigid, sunken boy

No older than I.

Afraid yet drawn to this shell,

Soulless.

I wondered, did his mother yet miss him?

Was no one seeking the boy astray? Slowly,

I leaned closer, not wanting him to be

Alone, detached within his fade.

And so, I sat by his side.

He might have been a school mate,

A friend, but passed through

Unknown,

Unsought,

Unclaimed.

And I allowed my hand to

Gently rest

Upon his shoulder and

Felt the cold,

The cold within, the cold

Neither should know.

It made me tremble.

I pulled my hand back rapidly,

Grasping it to ward off

The chill, cleanse the blunting,

But it was too late.

The bitter early frost is ruthless; once tasted,

It enters without remorse or care

For the waning.

-April 12, 2020, 1:41 AM

Behind the Wall

It's me, they say, behind

Where none can be

But they stay confined

So, none can see.

I see he and he through me.

I am she when no one's there.

I am here; I must be.

Breathless now with all I hear,

No one near.

Wild Eyes are soul-searching

Wild Eyes watching me.

Mild cries, somber from questions

Bringing me down.

Wild Eyes roll in passion.

Mild cries spoken through wild lies,

Savage now.

It's me, they say, behind

Where none can be

But they are confined

So, none can see.

Breathless now with all I hear,

No one near.

No one.

No.

-Approx. 1991

Still Winds

This year

Winter approached astern,

Obscured by temperance,

Clouded for the want.

Claiming leniency, winter was unforgiving.

Its still winds burn with

The shudders of February,

Contagions of March,

The butcher's bill, April,

And the flames of May.

Plainly visible 'neath the plating of gold,

Unrest is deafening in the chasm.

And the resistance is unyielding

From this dizzying height.

-June 2, 2020, 12:35 AM

Illegal

Paolo braved the First World War safely on American soil,

A stowaway on a New York-bound ship.

Just another W.O.P.

Leaving his wife and children for now, he knew,

He knew he'd go back for them. He knew,

She'd wait for him.

Stateside, Paolo ate from Manhattan trash and

Slept in Manhattan doorways.

Hiding, seeking work.

Just another W.O.P.

Paolo pledged allegiance in uniform, on Calvary
horseback;

The flood of the undocumented were welcomed in

For a price.

Join the Army and See the World.

As the sons of American workers died in trenches

On French and Italian fronts

Torn by phantasm

In the land of no man,

Each huddled son of afar

Lived the imperial bleed

In the suicide rush as

Just another W.O.P.

-November 11, 2018 – Armistice Centenary

Silent Seconds, Tender, Stark (for Laurie)

Earth.

Soft in sound, spacious ground,

Light of sky, breath of all.

Senses' song shimmers long;

Who am I to claim it for my own?

Glassine waters flowing through

Scent of summer's glare,

Stare down tomorrow's fall, forgotten freeze,

Ruptured soil still forces life anew for an

Eternal, daunting, quiet view.

Who but I to claim it for my own?

Taut moments in the dark,

Light of sky and nothing leads,

Silent seconds, tender, stark,

All we breathe and expression exceeds,

Wanton, nascent, savage need;

The one. The land. Sparse moments of yore.

All through the silken night with

My hands in your hair, I release myself through

Your being.

We melt away the outer, erasing lifelong hours,

Exposing all invisible, unseen.

And who am I to claim you for my own?

July 9, 2019, 11:45pm, Woodstock NY

Relentless (for Laurie)

Lost, still,

In the radiance of her eyes

Framed by such mesmerizing lips,

Singularly determined chin and flowing hair.

Lost, continuously,

In the strength of her being,

The stance of her every and

The creativity of confidence.

40 years—more!—have only allowed

The beauty to

Show, to grow, to flourish as my teenaged

Breathlessness melted into a sigh.

Still, the infectious smile, only made more alluring

By her knowing glance. And my rush of pulsation.

My date, my girl, my friend, my lover, my partner, my
wife.

My Laurie.

Lost, always, in her captivating green eyes, her

Scent, her sound, her touch and

Taste.

And I remain hopelessly swathed in

Reverence.

Eros, Eros, you are damned relentless...

-June 6, 2019, 1:14AM

The Poet's Constellation

The Words. The Words cut like incisors drawn

Over fragility. Passion-driven, the words cast

The new from antiquity and with

Grasps literary, bend, spindle and mold

Ambiguity.

The Words. The Words detect and malign,

Reject and respect the alien divine. With sublimity,

Terrorize and canonize and mutalatingly unify,

Indiscriminately holding desire by design. Drawing

Utter emotion to call out stagnation,

Daring to bring on the written

Revolution.

A life sentence of rhyming, a penance in hiding,

Phrasing is blinding over languid abidance of the

Mixed, the mired in unspoken abundance.

The Words.

The Words are all-knowing,

All-encompassing. Through letter and form,

Foreign and faithful, blurb and phrase liberate

Infinitum's infiltration. Sculpted, framed

In-sta-bil-iz-a-tion. A scalpeled whittling of

The Poet's Constellation.

Breathing planets surround flaming stars, blacking out

Light and pulsation,

Stellar sensation throbs

Climax-ation.

Peaceable mysteriosa, the words flagrantly

Sculpt the essence of mimosa,

Nightfall's espiritos cantata,

Kindred dreamworld of mythic steeds

The writer breeds

Transfigured persona.

The Words. The Words are spinning. Cyclones in space simply

Delivered. Thus idealized, it only figures. There's American

Configuration multiplied by blind fascination, a

Severing need for commutation.

Bleeding glad tidings, he's reading the writings,

Jesus Christ, the day rains perseveration! And, still,

And still,

    The holiest of grails remains

        Publication.

           99

-May 22, 2019, 12:34AM

Let's Meet At Lowenfel's!

Dwarfed by the towering landscape,

Lowenfel's Diner stands at the tango of 39th and
Broadway.

"Nighthawks" willed off the canvas,

It's gleam and streamers

Celebrated the christening with pre-war

Men in wide-lapel suits and felt hats and

Laughing ladies in seamed stockings.

Now it stands,

Draped in sepia.

"Let's Meet at Lowenfel's!"

The brass door handle, the black and white tile floor,

Bell Telephone booth stands still.

Misted, smoky interior, glass-encased counter.

The stool—chrome legs, sparkling red cushion--

Cash register and its

Opening bell.

No Sale.

South-bound lights toss winding streets,

My eyes blur as prisms tatter mirrored panels

And the burgeoning traffic claims Broadway.

Max Of 10th Ave

Max had a small office,

A tiny corner office in an old building,

Pre-War (possibly Civil);

Crossroads of 41st and 10$^{th.}$

Like something from a Dashiell Hammett,

It lurked on the dark side:

Black and white tile lobby,

Shadowy halls in brilliant grays,

Beveled, smoked glass office doors,

Transoms above.

> Third-floor, right turn off the elevator.
>
> Sharp left, end of the hall.
>
> "Suite" 307, *M. Levitt, Video and Film*
>
> There's Max,
>
> Max peering over dusty wire-rim glasses,
>
> On the phone with 42nd Street's finest distributer,
>
> Holding his head and nodding.

All belly and rumpled shirt,

Stacked behind his desk.

Atop it, invoices in hapless piles,

Overpowering fluorescent lamp and

Catalogs of plain brown covers

Next to an overfilled ashtray,

Partially eaten meatball hero,

And a warming Dr. Pepper.

Sitting

Amidst buckling shelves,

Burdened cabinets and

Spread-eagled, spike-heeled

Bondage scenes

In full color

Just behind his head.

All in a day's work.

Max, looking over dusty wire-rim eyeglasses,

Lenses reflecting fluorescent glare

Like a pair of glowing headlights.

Licking a fingertip, he

Flips through a catalog,

The models,

Stacked, behind, burlesque.

Atop them, prurience in hapless piles,

Overpowering, unscented camp with

Cat-housed, stained and bound lovers

Next to the overfilled,

And partially eaten.

Warming.

BREATHE

Breathe, she said.

I stood and saw strangely

The racing, the

Constriction.

The dizzying moment eternal.

Staring ahead, I saw none and

In listening, only silence spoke back.

And it overwhelmed.

Breathe, she said.

Fists reddened, pupils become outsized black pools.

Core pulsations drum arhythmic batterie

Over an imaginary mambo.

And breath is left to intermission.

-April 22, 2019, 11:58PM

The Front: for John Reed

Loud discussion and siren scuttle

City lore.

In the farther contain, there were others betrayed and

At land's end, one forgets any at all remained.

        I breathed deeply the solitude, inhaling the scent

            Of turnings past. The winding staircase

      Of heavy iron encasement stood yards from the port.

                And miles from equity.

The elevator to the rail line, no longer ran

And this terrible length was the only means upward.

I climbed with caution and determination.

Higher, higher, toward the track,

Where one might catch the next car northeast, over the
river; away.

So, I climbed.

             Looking down, I dared to, ground

      Wet with rising tide. The moon reigned full through
                    afternoon's sky

      Where it shone brighter and fuller than before.

Stepping off the last of the metal stairs, I took the
platform.

There were no other passengers, no others

To add the polyrhythms of dancing pulsations

To the structure on high.

I looked downward to see the sizzling swamp,

Overstepping the yellow caution stripes on the station
floor.

Yes, I'd laid dormant before such awakening.

And I moved, then, to the advance.

The advance.

-June 2, 2020, 1:02 AM.

Repelling Ghosts:

for Kenneth Fearing and for Jean-Michel Basquiat

Listening.

It's something writers just do.

The world without,

Sans modesty,

Wrestles within and

Flirts question after question.

Armed with pen and tablet,

We emerge, absorbing

Bits and slices and cells

To compel the drama.

The players are spirits begone;

Their resonance

Splashes eyes, colors

The breast, and casts

Painted--wildly

Painted--shadows.

It's but the hand of the poet,

Through ions

Of literary lore,

That repels ghosts and

Penetrates phantoms.

Words Shaped onto the Hollow

From well inside, the words shaped,

   Seeking form and phrase.

   Night guiding, shadows reached outward,

   In, as I sat embraced by

   A black velvet darkness,

   And no longer recognized

   The long forgot,

   Daylight's denial of

   Seasons lingering somebody.

      From well within, the verse:

      Obscured, yet simply read,

      Plotted by faces reflected

      And weary of light.

      And still, the words,

      The words shaped

      The words shaped onto the hollow,

      The spare, the baring, despairing quiet.

        It takes what it will,

        Demands all and

        Returns every.

     Syllables of song, the moments flowed through

Wonder, pulsation and breath, halted breath.

This poured from my fingers and cast new selves
onto old

Till dawn's break and

Day's ascend.

And then I slept.

-June 8, 2018, 1:40 AM

A Peripheral Haunting

Trevor Baudelaire never liked looking down and seeing
busy designs;

They were so distracting.

Each time he'd begin to focus on the work, the shirt

Kept grabbing at his attention.

Gnawing at his attention.

At first it was subtle, a distant whispering.

And then more pronounced.

He tried to keep his eyes on the book, but

The words kept going out of focus as the shirt

Forced its way into his view.

Again and again.

With intent, Trevor stared back at it,

The cursed thing,

Trying to beat the careening, colliding design

At its own game.

But the wave of nausea resumed its command

Over both stomach and throat.

He rubbed at his eyes with outstretched palms

And wiped the perspiration coating his face.

Sitting back, Trevor stared at the ceiling, pensively.

There was a time, he would tell others,

When festive navy blue was at least tolerable.

-April 15, 2019 1:32 AM

The Late-Night Breakfast Special

'Smith Street Eats' is always open.

It's stated in neon.

After-hours as high noon, Hopper's New York,

now.

The coffee is a steaming, shining thing of

Darkest black.

The night manager, Alexander Alexander, is

Often asked about his name,

    With a roll in his R explains:

        "Used to be *Aleksander Aleksander.*

            I shorrrtened it".

The juke plays, but none can hear.

The bus-box moans stainless steel as

    June Christy bellows in silver cool.

        "My friend, you come so late.

          I thought maybe

      You start cooking or something crazy"

Denying the cooking rumor, I take

the booth up front and request the

Turkey Sloppy Joe on toast,

        Rice on the side to soak up the
grease.

        "Hey, grease eees acquired taaaste",

Alex says, taking an eye off his crossword puzzle.

"And coffee, rright?"

He didn't wait for an answer.

       "Seeelvia, make my late friend a Brreakfast
                  Special!".

      ......

The coffee is a steaming,

Shining thing pouring

Darkest pitch

This black hour....

And June Christy cries loneliest,

An unrequited prayer

For the sacred

Night dweller.

-*June 2, 2019, 3:02 AM*

The Stark, Bleached Whiteness

In the hushed attic, strains of light

Betray windows battened,

Tracing effects into the dusk,

Long cherished and long forgotten.

I, a child; mother afar,

No reach, no breath for the calling.

Closed and shadowed, this dreamscape,

Tall tales of fortune and fallen.

Amid the still and stifled air,

Dear holdings of long past lore,

A black marble lioness stares above,

Reclining on belly and claw.

Its human head, mouth agape,

Sings in darkest glimmer,

Carved hair bobbed high, moons burn sight,

Turn one with shining pillars.

Eyes closed tight and face forlorn,

Sleepless, the hours belie.

I, as in youth, paint over the dawn,

In name, we testify.

Split shutters part the sordid air,

Baring the gospel blindness.

And mother eclipsed with the essence of spring,

Into the stark, bleached whiteness.

-May 23, 2020, 2:02 am

For Carmela Pietaro, 2/8/1935-5/21/2020

Becoming One

(led by quotes from the children of Sprout U, Newark NJ)

Wisdom of the age pours forth,
Multi-colored water paints
Spread over surface
Far too wide to see.

> *"Watching our kings and queens pass,*
> *The officers say they…"*

Wisdom of the age pours forth
Like song from those too young,
Too young to recall the hurt,
The hurt of---of repetition,

> *"The officers say they fear for their lives, NO"*

The chagrin of
Of disillusion.
Vexations
Of failure.

> *"I miss my mom.*
> *I miss my brother"*

Too young,
Far too young to feel the
Miscarriage, the haunt of
Relent, throbbing constraint.
The poisoning.

> *"The officers say,*
> *"The officers say they fear*
> *They fear for their lives, NO.*
> ***They fear OURS.***

Lucky they, too old,
Far too old,
Too old to
ACCEPT.
To ACCEPT.

> *"The quarantine is overwhelming and*
> *Unexpected.*
> *It makes me worry about*
> *The wellbeing of the earth"*

Where others have painfully,
Where others have painfully adapted,
Adapted to

> *"The officers say they fear for their lives, NO.*
> *They fear ours.*
> *They fear our excellence, they fear,*
> *They fear our grace,*
> *Our smarts,*
> *They fear"*

The disconcert.
The space we live in,
All live in...

> *"The pandemic makes me feel upset because*
> *I can not.*
> *I cannot hug,*
> *I cannot..."*

Where others have painfully,
Where others have painfully adapted,
Adapted to,

> *"I hope we all stay safe.*
> *I hope,*
> *I hope"*

Painfully forgotten.

"I hope they are ok"

Far too old, they are,
Far too old to…
Far too old.

*"It's not fair. It's not fair.
Black Lives Matter
And always will"*

They, who will lead our way.

*"We should
Be one"*

-June 9, 2020, 8:11pm

The Continuum

They're lost in the hours,

Broken into fragments,

These seconds.

Where time once labored,

It races to a blur,

Over-wound hands obscuring faces.

Through grinding gears,

And gabbling sprockets,

Each moment that was,

Continues.

And the shadows are bathed in the richest of grays,

In a spectrum wider,

Wider than the eyes will ever see.

###

ABOUT ATMOSPHERE PRESS

Atmosphere Press is an independent, full-service publisher for excellent books in all genres and for all audiences. Learn more about what we do at atmospherepress.com.

We encourage you to check out some of Atmosphere's latest releases, which are available at Amazon.com, Barnes & Noble, and via order from your local bookstore:

Big Man Small Europe, poetry by Tristan Niskanen
In the Cloakroom of Proper Musings, a lyric narrative by Kristina Moriconi
Lucid_Malware.zip, poetry by Dylan Sonderman
The Unordering of Days, poetry by Jessica Palmer
It's Not About You, poetry by Daniel Casey
A Dream of Wide Water, poetry by Sharon Whitehill
Radical Dances of the Ferocious Kind, poetry by Tina Tru
The Woods Hold Us, poetry by Makani Speier-Brito
My Cemetery Friends: A Garden of Encounters at Mount Saint Mary in Queens, New York, nonfiction and poetry by Vincent J. Tomeo
Report from the Sea of Moisture, poetry by Stuart Jay Silverman
The Enemy of Everything, poetry by Michael Jones
The Stargazers, poetry by James McKee
The Pretend Life, poetry by Michelle Brooks
Minnesota and Other Poems, poetry by Daniel N. Nelson
Interviews from the Last Days, sci-fi poetry by Christina Loraine
the oneness of Reality, poetry by Brock Mehler

ABOUT THE AUTHOR

Photo: Sherry Rubel

JOHN PIETARO is a writer, poet, spoken word artist and musician from Brooklyn NY. Columnist/critic of *the NYC Jazz Record,* curator of the West Village Word series at Café Bohemia, and director of the Dissident Arts Festival, his latest published work, *The Mercer Stands Burning: Night Poems* (Atmosphere Press) was completed during the covid-19 lockdown as was short fiction collection, *Enduring Neon Moments.* In partnership with photographer Sherry Rubel, Pietaro is currently engaged in a study of NYC's downtown experimental and post-punk underground arts, *Beneath the Underground.* He is also in the final stage of non-fiction collection *On the Creative Front: Essays on the Culture of Liberation.* In 2019, he launched poetry chapbook *Smoke Rings.*

Other recent credits include several entries in the upcoming edition of *The Encyclopedia of the American Left* (Verso 2021), poetry or fiction for anthologies Heroes Are Gangleaders *Gianthology, Who Are We?* (UK: Willowdown), *Father and I* (Wingless Dreamer), *Poems from the Lockdown* (UK: Willowdown), *Il Biglietto 2* (Italy: Sibello), and journals *Sensitive Skin, Lucent Dreaming, Howling Press, Headline Press, Rye, Genre: Urban Arts, Ovunque Siamo, International Human Rights Arts Festival* and *Harbinger Asylum.* Pietaro also penned contemporary proletarian fiction collection *Night People & Other Tales of Working New York* (2013) and contributed a chapter to Paul Buhle and Harvey Pekar's *SDS: A Graphic History* (Hill & Wang 2007). Pietaro is a contributing writer to *the Wire* (UK), *Z, the Nation, Please Kill Me, the Village Sun, Counter Punch, People's World, All About Jazz, Political Affairs, Fifth Estate* and others.

A guest speaker at Left Forum and the Vision Festival, Pietaro has been a featured reader at Great Weather for Media's Spoken Word Sundays, the Workers United Film Festival, the UpSurge JazzPoetry Festival and numerous other venues. As a percussionist, guitarist and/or spoken word artist, he's collaborated with Allen Ginsberg, Pete Seeger, Amina Baraka, Karl Berger, Steve Dalachinsky, Ras Moshe, Erika Dagnino, Puma Perl and many more. He fronts post-punk neo-Beat ensemble Shadows and spoken word/free jazz quartet the Red Microphone; the former recorded debut album *And I Became of the Dark* in November 2020; the latter collaborated with Amina Baraka on *Amina Baraka & the Red Microphone* (ESP-Disk, 2017). Ms. Baraka also performed Pietaro's "Her Side of the Road" as a dramatic reading with music in 2017. Pietaro is a member of the Author's Guild, the Jazz Journalists Association, Academy of American Poets, the National Writers Union, the Poetry Society of New York and the International Society of Improvised Music.

Website: JohnPietaro.com

Blog: TheCulturalWorker.blogspot.com